OOR WULLIE

D. C. Thomson & Co. Ltd. GLASGOW, LONDON, DUNDEE. £1·40

OOR WULLIE- A great wee sport!

When Wullie kicks a fitba,
 It rockets through the air.
And there's nae doobt, as you can see,
 He's sure a " smashing " player!

Now here's Oor Wullie racing
 In the Buckie Brae Grand Prix.
He looks a sure-fire winner till
 His fower wheels shrink tae three!

At " hammer-throwing " Wull's a champ—
 It's one event he'll win!
(But what's inside that piggy bank?
 Twa washers and a pin!)

When sprinting, Wull's a wonder—
 He'll tak' on a' the rest.
Wi' a' the practice that HE gets,
 He's bound tae be the best!

At cricket, Wullie eyes the ba'
 And swings his bat at it.
But ach, he's beaten by the bounce—
 It's the ba' that scores a " hit "!

**Aye, Wullie is a great wee sport,
 A champion through and through.
And when it comes to winning laughs,
 Oor lad knows what to do!**

Printed and Published in Great Britain by D. C. THOMSON & CO., LTD., 185 Fleet Street, London EC4A 2HS.
© D. C. THOMSON & CO., LTD., 1982.
ISBN 0 85116 269 X

It's five-past nine, and Wullie's late—

And guess who's waiting at the gate!

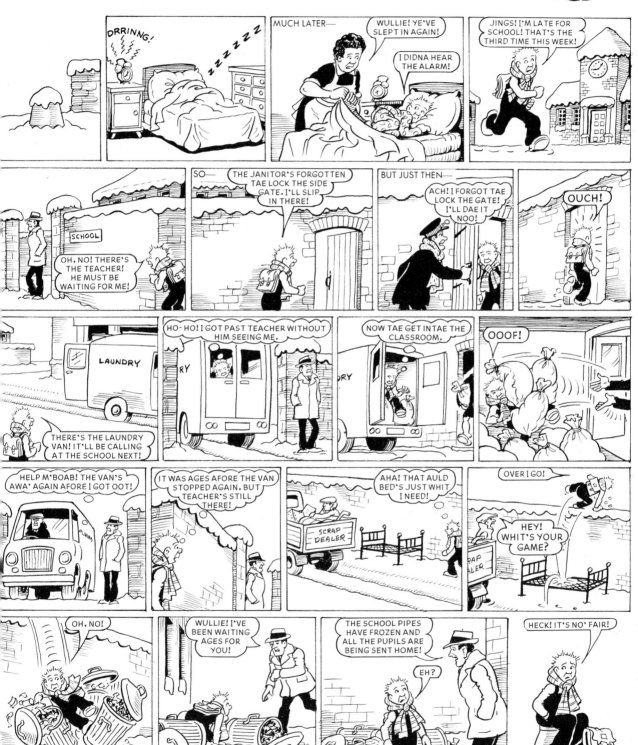

Laughter treats—

With blankets and sheets!

. . . but that padlock and chain—

Are just a pain!

Wullie gets a fish then he—

Suffers a CATastrophe!

See Wullie scamper at the double—

To miss a bucketload of trouble!

BRING IN SOME COAL IN YER BUCKET, WULLIE!

RICHT, MA!

BUT—

WULLIE! LOOK AT THE MESS YE'RE MAKIN'!

AWA' WI' YE!

NO WONDER I MADE A MESS! I'VE A HOLE IN MY BUCKET!

THEN—

...AND THE FLAIR WAS COVERED IN COAL DUST!

I'LL SEE WULLIE ABOUT THAT.

I'M AWA' TILL PAW COOLS AFF! I'LL GET SOMETHING TAE REPAIR MY BUCKET.

WULLIE'S HOOSE

'SO—

I'D LIKE A REPAIR KIT, PLEASE.

IS IT FOR A BIKE TYRE, AN AIR-BED...

NO! IT'S FOR A BUCKET.

WHY, YE CHEEKY...

BICYCLE SHOP

GET OUT! AND DON'T WASTE MY TIME!

I'LL TRY IN HERE.

CHEMIST

I'D LIKE A LARGE BANDAGE, PLEASE.

OH, HAS THERE BEEN AN ACCIDENT?

I KNOW FIRST-AID.

I'LL HELP TOO!

CHEMIST

ER—I'LL NO' BOTHER, THANKS!

SHORTLY—

I'D LIKE THE BIGGEST PLUG YE'VE GOT!

ALL SIZES OF BATH & BASIN PLUGS IN STOCK

WASHERS

HERE WE ARE, SONNY! THAT'LL BE £1.

YE'RE JOKING! I COULDNA AFFORD THAT!

ALL OF

THEN—

HMM! THAT'S AN IDEA!

MAKE YOUR CHAIRS AS GOOD AS NEW WITH 'LOOSE COVERS'

I'D LIKE A LOOSE COVER FOR MY SEAT.

YES! NOW IS IT A COUCH OR AN EASY CHAIR?

NEITHER! IT'S A BUCKET!

WE DO NOT COVER BUCKETS! OUT!

WULLIE! SO YE'RE HOME AT LAST!

WULLIE'S HOOSE

I'VE GOT SOMETHING FOR YE!

A NEW BUCKET! I'M SORRY! IT WAS ME THAT PUT A HOLE IN YER LAST ONE!

Fat Bob's "barking" is first-rate—

That other dog thinks it's just GRReat!

One wee " *bloodhound* ", *mini-size—*

Gives Oor Wull a big surprise!

 THERE'S MURDOCH! HE SEEMS TAE BE LOOKING FOR CLUES TO SOME BIG CRIME OR OTHER!

 HELLO, MURDOCH! I CAN SEE YE'RE ON A BIG JOB. CAN I HELP? / NO — ER — I CANNA INVOLVE THE PUBLIC.

 ACH! I'LL SEE WHIT I CAN DAE TAE HELP HIM ONYWAY!

 THERE'S A SUSPICIOUS-LOOKING LAD! IF I CAN GET A LOOK AT HIS FACE, I CAN IDENTIFY HIM LATER.

 THIS'LL MAK' HIM LOOK UP!

 YOWCH! / CECIL! WHERE DO YOU THINK YOU'RE GOING? I TOLD YOU TO CUT THE GRASS!

 YE INTERFERIN' LITTLE . . . / I'M AFF!

 THESE FOOTPRINTS COULD BELONG TAE THE CRIMINAL MURDOCH'S AFTER!

 WHIT ARE YOU DAEIN', WULL? / STUDYING FOOTPRINTS!

 I'LL HELP! / OUCH!

 THAT'S ANITHER FOOTPRINT FOR YE TAE STUDY!

 I'VE BORROWED GRANNY GREEN'S MAGNIFYING GLASS TAE LOOK FOR CLUES!

 YIKE!

 UGH! / HELP!

 S-SORRY, MISTER, BUT I SAW A BIG UGLY SNAKE!

 SNAKE? ITS JIST A FAT WORM! / OH, NO! THE GLASS MADE IT LOOK HUGE!

 I DINNA HAE A BLOODHOUND, BUT MAYBE JEEMY WILL SNIFF SOMETHING OOT!

 HE'S GOT THE SCENT O' SOMETHING! I CAN SEE A PARCEL UNDER THERE!

 CHEESE SANDWICHES? YOU'VE FOUND THEM, WULLIE! THAT'S WHIT I'VE BEEN LOOKING FOR! THEY FELL OOT O' MY SADDLE-BAG!

 ACH! AN' YOU LET ME THINK YOU WERE ON A BIG CASE!

Wullie's ploys are really grand—

It's clear to all they beat the band!

Oor Wullie likes his game of tennis—

Until it's ruined by this menace!

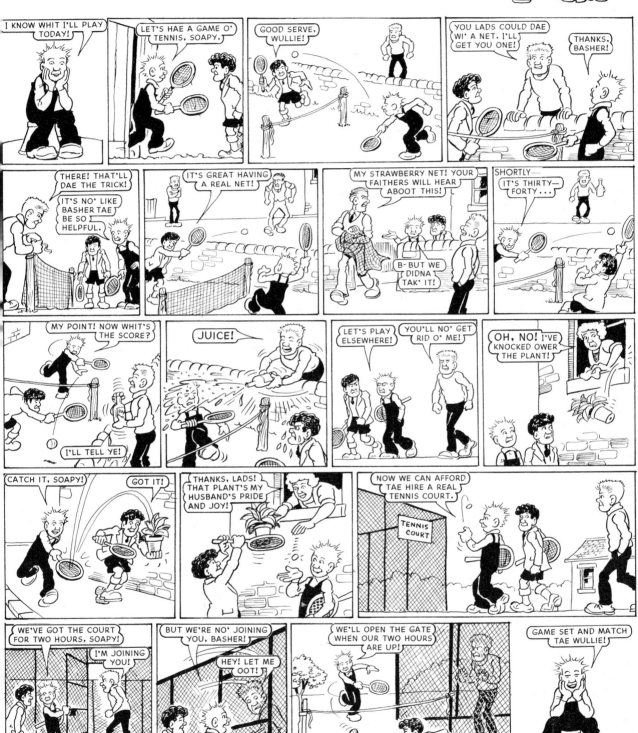

Wull wants to get his hair trimmed, but—
He'd rather see the PRICES cut!

Heap big fun with Wullie now—

He's a real smart chief, and " how!"

Things for Wull go far from right—

It's here to see, in BLACK and WHITE!

See who's still around to play—

When Wull's pals are on holiday!

See the glint in Wullie's eyes—

He's got some smashing " bargain buys!"

As a joker, Wull's the best—

And so he plans a birthday jest.

Who cares if the rain pours doon?—

Wullie's the happiest lad in toon!

Life at Wullie's home's no joke—

Sometimes, there's just no pleasing folk!

Teacher, dentist or a doc—
Each job Wull chooses brings a shock!

Wullie's grin just grows and grows—

What's the reason? Murdoch knows!

Wull's an EGGSpert when it comes—

To Easter fun with his three chums!

Soapy and Wullie will make you hoot—

When they start to muck aBOOT!

Oor Wullie's bandaged, head to toe —

Is he upset? Just look below!

What's this? Murdoch on the run?—

Whatever has the bobby done?

Imagine Wullie as a star—
With flashy suit and great big car!

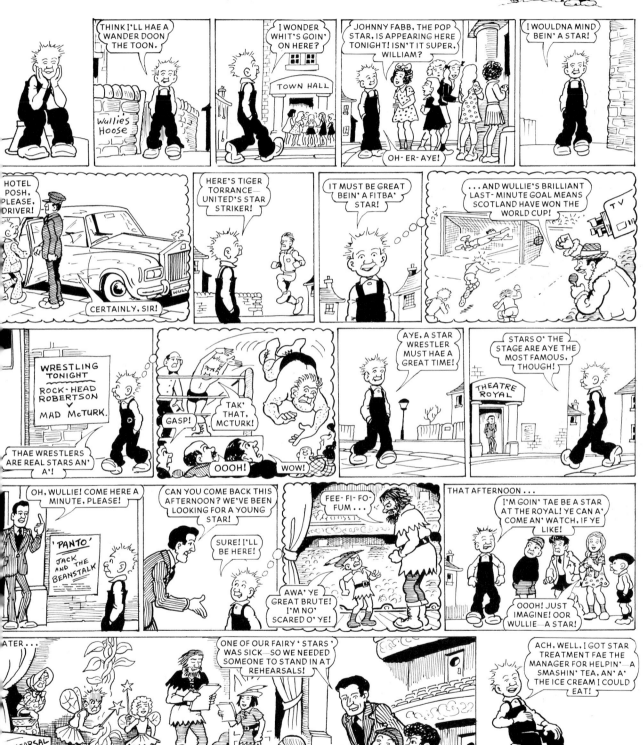

Oor Wullie tries out every wheeze—

To end up with a sniff and sneeze!

No wonder no one wants to know—

When Wullie wants to earn some dough!

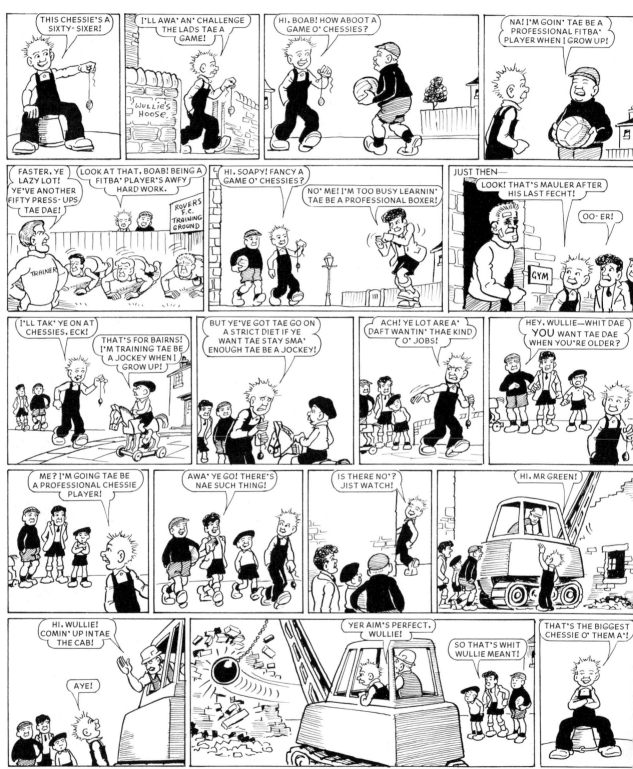

The chums soon wish they hadn't jested—

When it seems that they're arrested!

  WE HIVNAE PLAYED ANY TRICKS ON P.C. MURDOCH FOR AGES. LET'S HAE SOME FUN.

 SO COME QUICK! THERE'S A STICK-UP ROOND THE CORNER!

 BAH! IT'S JUST A BILL-STICKER!

YE CHEEKY SCAMPS!

 LATER— HEY! I'VE JUST SEEN TWO MEN DIGGING THEIR WAY INTO A BANK!

 NO! NOT THAT BANK! FARTHER ON!

 THERE THEY ARE! THE RIVER BANK! WHY, YE . . .

 LATER STILL— P.C. MURDOCH! I'VE JUST SEEN TWO HOLD-UPS IN THE HIGH STREET.

 TWO? THIS IS SERIOUS!

 THERE'S ONE! A TRAFFIC HOLD-UP!

 AND THERE'S THE OTHER! AULD JOCK'S BRACES HAVE BURST AND HE'S HOLDING UP HIS BREEKS!

 HO-HO!

 THAT AFTERNOON— THE ROVERS SHOULD WIN TODAY, EH, LADS?

 BUT JUST THEN— STOP RIGHT THERE! P.C. MURDOCH!

 IN YE GET! BUT IT WAS ONLY A JOKE . . .

 WE'RE FOR IT NOW! AYE! AND WE'LL MISS THE MATCH.

 SOON— OUT YE GET! ARE WE AT THE POLICE STATION?

 NO! YE'RE AT THE ROVERS' GROUND! I'M ON DUTY AT THE MATCH TODAY!

 COME AWAY THE BOYS!

 ACH! MURDOCH'S A REAL SPORT!

Wullie quickly makes it plain—

That windae-cleanin' is a " pane "!

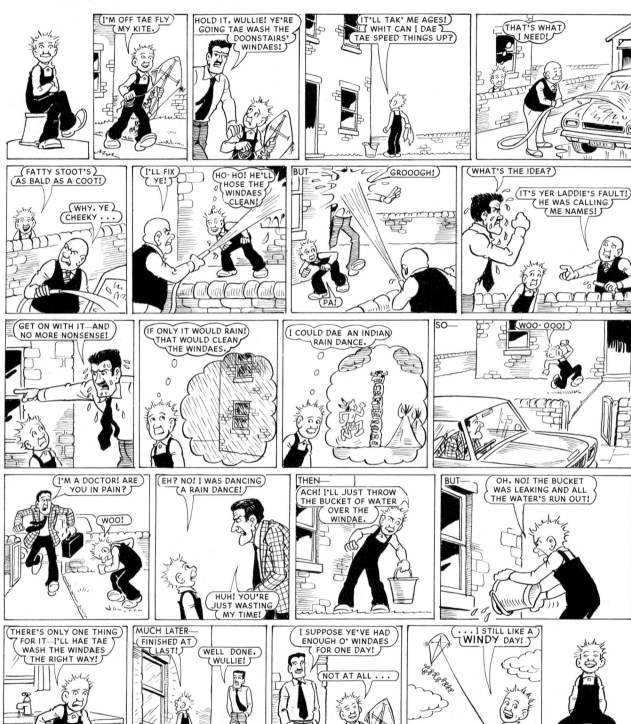

Wi' magnet Wull goes intae action—

And soon becomes a big " attraction "!

At crafty ploys oor lad's a smasher—

He sorts oot Bully Briggs AND Basher!

Nae wonder Wullie's feelin' dopey—

All his plans are really " ropey "!

When Wullie tries his latest trick—

He finds Pa has a BONE to pick!

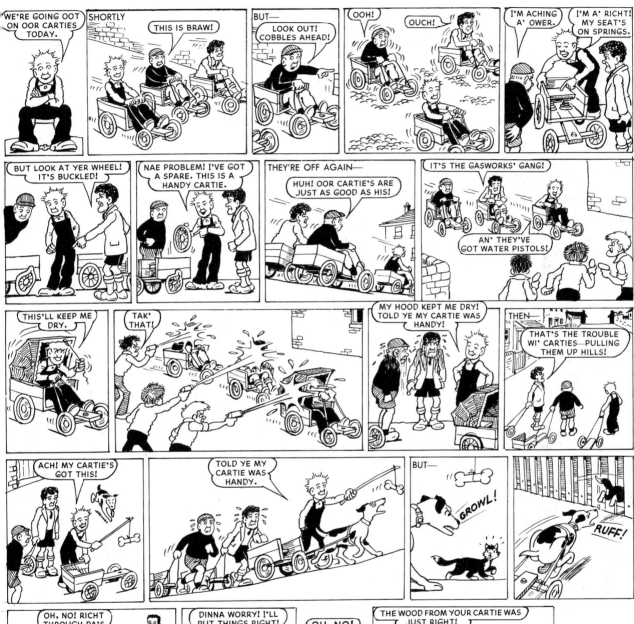

Footprints here—and footprints there—

And they all lead oor lad nowhere!

There's trouble when the teacher sees
The bike clips on Wull's dungarees!

Whichever sport Oor Wullie chooses—

There's one thing sure—he always loses!

Roll up, roll up for a circus thrill—

But poor wee Wullie's had his fill!

Lots o' shocks—

Wi' curly locks!

Wellies, waders and shiny boots—

And loads and loads of laughter hoots!

WULLIE'S ON HOLIDAY!

IT WAS NICE O' MY PAL, JIM, TAE INVITE US TAE SPEND A FEW DAYS ON HIS FARM.

BUT YE'LL NEED A NEW PAIR O' BOOTS. YE'VE HAD THAT PAIR FOR AGES!

AW, PA! I LIKE THESE ANES!

WE'RE OFF TAE THE VILLAGE, JIM!

SOON—
MY LADDIE NEEDS A NEW PAIR O' BOOTS.

TRY THIS PAIR ON, SONNY.

HELP! THEY'RE SO SHINY, THEY'RE BLINDING ME!

WELL WHAT ABOUT WELLINGTONS?

THEY LOOK FINE! TRY WALKING IN THEM!

OOF!

ER . . . I FORGOT TO CUT THE STRING BETWEEN THEM.

HMPH! WELLIES ARE OOT!

I'M SURE WE MUST HAVE SOMETHING FOR YOU . . . DO YOU GO FISHING?

AYE!

WELL, WE SELL WADERS! TRY THEM ON!

BUT—
I'LL NO' GET FAR LIKE THIS!

HMM! TOO BIG I'M AFRAID.

THEN—
LISTEN . . . MUTTER . . . MUMBLE . . .

OF COURSE WE SELL THEM, SIR!

RIGHT, WULLIE! BACK TO THE FARM!

WHAT'S PA GOT IN MIND?

BOOTS & SHOES

JIM WILL HELP ME!

OH, NO!

PA'S GOING TAE PUT HORSESHOES ON MY BOOTS!

BUT SOON—
WHIT A RELIEF!

PA JUST GOT HIS PAL TAE HAMMER TACKETS INTAE THEM!

A length o' string and an auld tin can—

That's a' you need for a " rattling " good plan!

Wull fools his Pa, and teacher, too—

But things look bad for you-know-who!

Is Wullie ill, or going saft?—

His chums think so—but he's no daft!

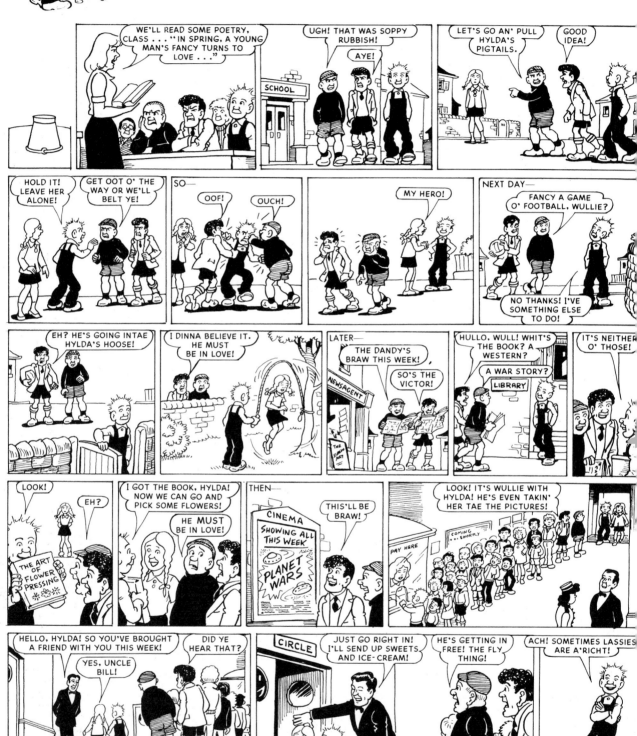

Wullie's got cakes on his mind—

But here's a sponge of another kind!

This rugby ball's a funny sight—

But soon it is EGGSactly right!

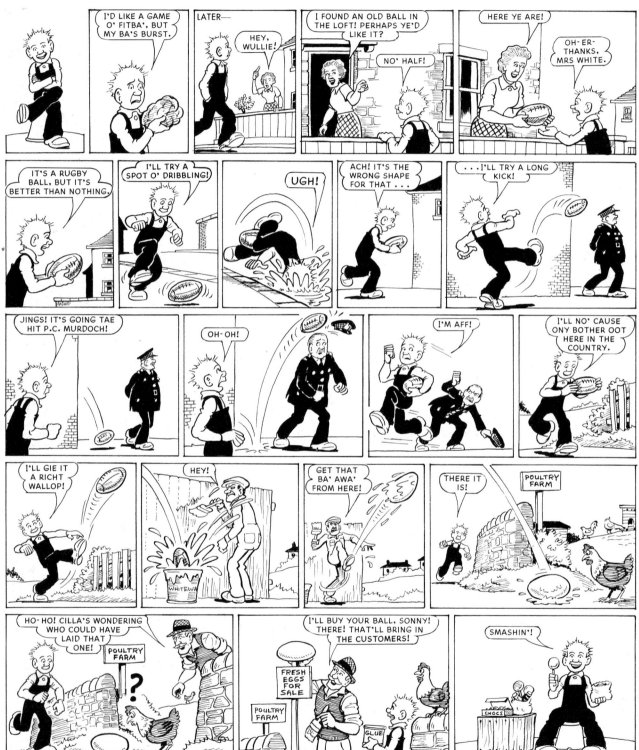

Across that fence see Wullie climb—

He's going tae hae a RIPPING time!

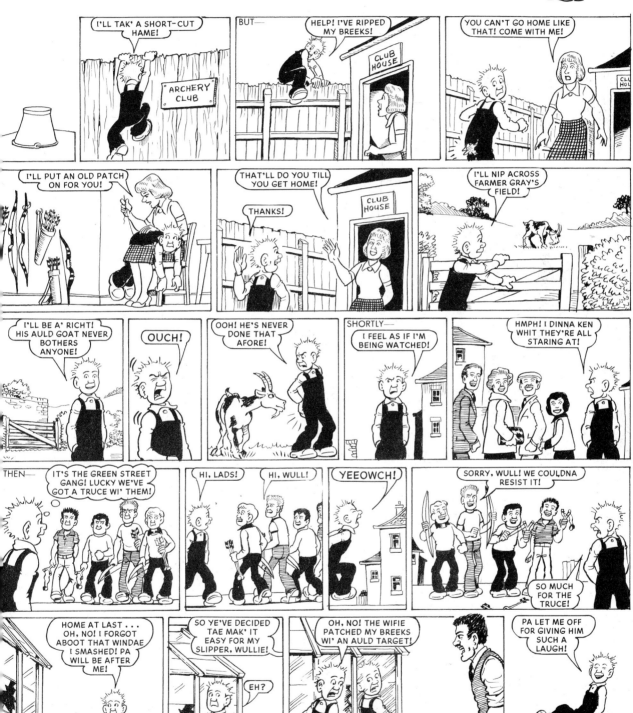

" *Finders keepers!*" *says oor chum—*

But this find makes him really glum!

JINGS! TEN PENCE!

I SAW YE FIND THAT! HAND IT OVER!

YE'RE NOT ON!

I'M AFF!

I'LL HIDE IN THERE!

WAREHOUSE

I HEAR HIM RUNNING PAST.

WHERE'S HE GONE?

WAREHOUSE

THEN—

THIS MUST BE THE CRATE FOR FINLAND!

FINLAND! BUT I DINNA WANT TAE GO THERE!

OOF!

I'D BETTER SCRAM AFORE THEY BOX MY EARS!

TIME TO SPEND MY CASH!

THAT'LL BE TEN PENCE!

WHAT'S THIS? A FOREIGN COIN!

EH?

GET OOT O' HERE, YE WEE TRICKSTER!

WELL, IF IT'S NO' WORTH ANYTHING I'LL HAE SOME FUN WI' IT!

HERE'S BOAB AND SOAPY!

LOOK! TEN PENCE!

IT ROLLED DOON HERE!

THEN—

I'VE FOUND FIVE PENCE!

AN' HERE'S SOME COPPERS! THERE'S A SMA' FORTUNE DOON THERE!

SOON—

HO-HO! WHIT A TREASURE TROVE! I'LL SEE IF THERE'S ANY MONEY LEFT!

BUT—

ACH! THAT FOREIGN COIN AGAIN!

LOOKS LIKE I'M STUCK WI' YOU!

Oor Wullie's acting awfy funny—
He doesnae want his pocket money!

It's the brawest thing they've ever seen—

When Wullie takes on Grouchie Greene!

You'll never guess what—

He should have bought!

Pa's money's safe, or so it seems—

But one BAD shot upsets Pa's schemes!

Just tak' a look below and this'll—

Show why Ma's brush mak's folk " bristle "!

A peaceful day? That's what Pa thinks—

Until he joins his son's high jinks!

Pa thinks Oor Wullie's tellin' fibs—

But here's a TRUE tale from His Nibs!

It doesna need a clock tae chime—

Before Oor Wullie knows the time!

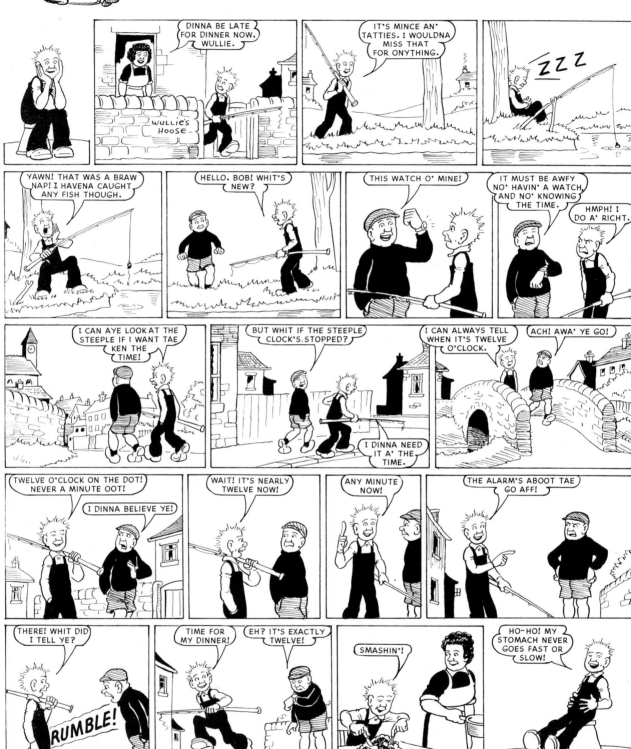

He's the best wee pet—

Wull could ever get!

False moustache or pogo stick—

This doorman sees through every trick!

Here's a load of smiles and frowns—
With Wullie's week of ups-and-downs!

He's the star o' the team—

But it's just one long dream!

Oor Wullie isn't pleased to find—

A " ringer " of another kind!

Oh, jings! Just see Oor Wullie's face—

When he meets folk from outer space!

Into hiding see Wull go—

Oor laddie's really LION low!

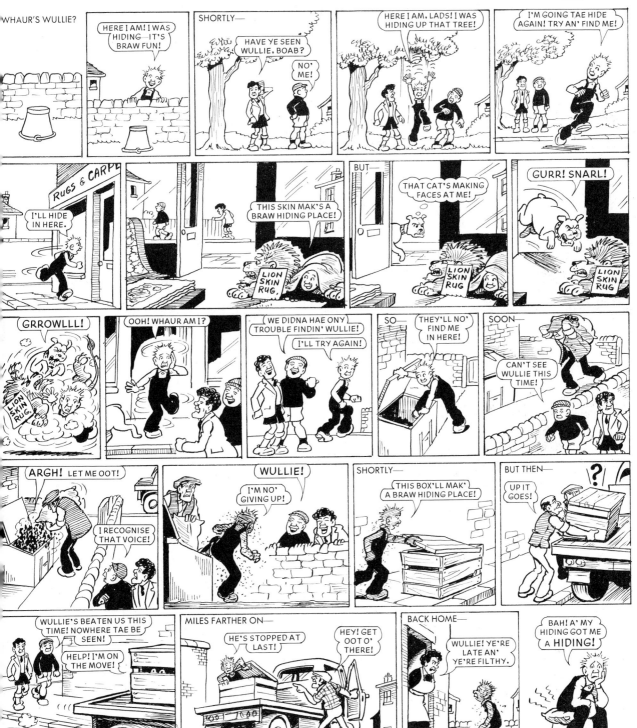

Wullie's ploys will mak' you smile—

When he tries chairs o' every style!

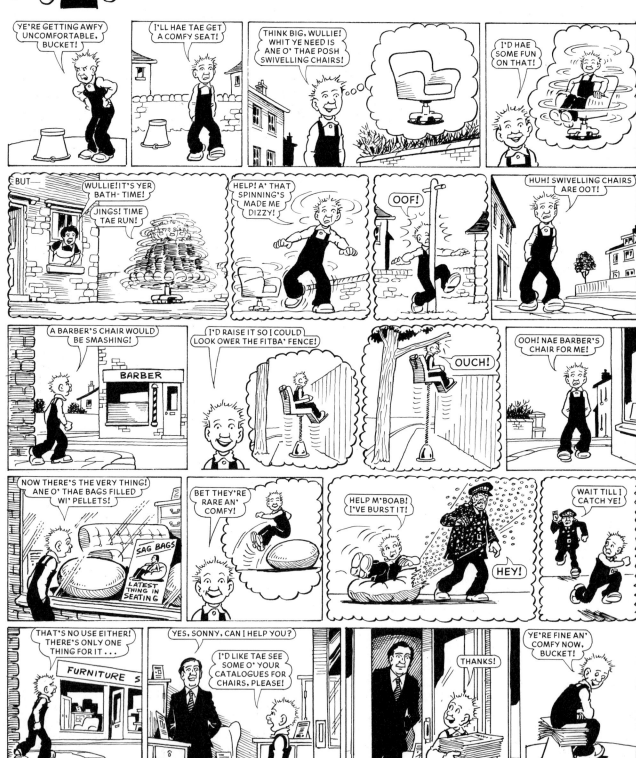

Look at what Oor Wullie's found—

His new pal's a muckle hound!

The day ANOTHER Gran'paw Broon—
Went wanderin' aroond the toon!

Michty me! There's something wrong—
Wullie's arms are four-feet long!

  *IT'S FROM YOUR COUSIN LILLY, WULLIE! SHE'S COMING TAE VISIT US.*

 *SHE CANNA SEE YE IN THESE AWFY-LOOKIN' DUNGAREES. SHE AYE WEARS THE LATEST FASHIONS!* — *BUT, MA...*

 *NAE ARGUIN'! WE'RE GETTING YOU SOME NEW CLOTHES.*

 *NOW STAY HERE, WULLIE, WHILE I FIND AN ASSISTANT.*

SHORTLY—

 *WULLIE...HE'S VANISHED!*

 THEN— *WULLIE! COME BACK THIS INSTANT!* — *TAM! THAT'S NO' A DUMMY.*

 *I'D LIKE A PAIR OF TROUSERS FOR MY LADDIE.*

 *NOW IF THE LITTLE GENTLEMAN WILL JUST PUT THIS TAPE MEASURE ROUND HIS WAIST.*

 *SIXTY-THREE INCHES...EH?*

 *THE WEE MONKEY'S PUT THE TAPE ROOND THE PILLAR.*

 *WELL, IF HE'LL JUST TRY THESE ON FOR SIZE!*

 *THEY'RE OWER SMALL ROOND THE WAIST.* — *HMM...*

  *WHIT'S THIS?* — *A CUSHION! SO THEY DO FIT!*

 *WE'LL NEED A JERSEY TAE GO WI' THE BREEKS!*

 *HERE'S A SMART LITTLE NUMBER!* — *UGH!*

 *LOOK! THE SLEEVES ARE OWER SHORT!*

 *LET'S SEE!*

 *DUMMY ARMS! YE CANNA FOOL ME!*

 *LE'S GO...* — *COO-EE, AUNTY!*

 *OH, HELLO, LILLY! FANCY MEETING YOU HERE! I WAS JUST BUYING A NEW RIG-OUT TO VISIT YOU!*

 *LIKE IT? IT'S THE LATEST STYLE!* — *DUNGAREES!*

 *WOMEN—HUH!*

Oor Wullie's no' a lad to quit—

That's a fact! You can BANK on it!

. . . but poor Wullie's floored—

By THIS notice board!

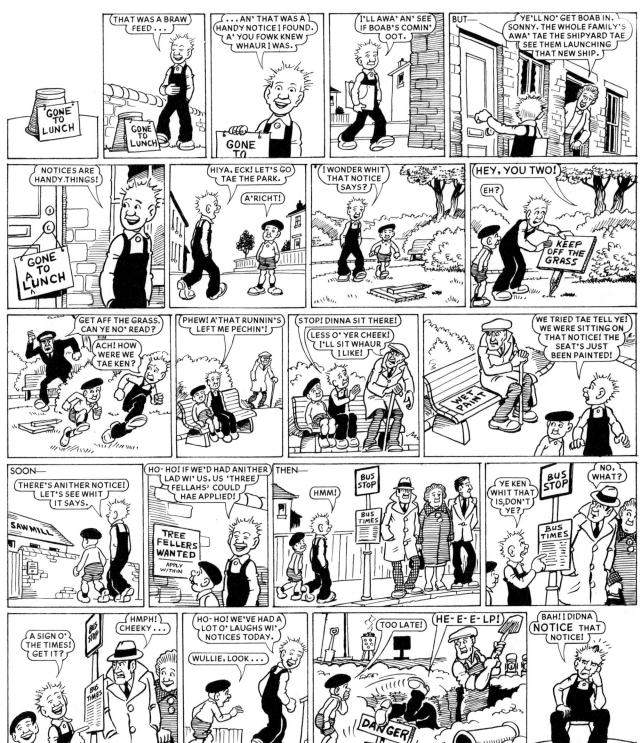

As half-past twelve at last draws near—

There's one sound Wullie waits to hear!

This garden roller weighs a ton—

But pulling it can be good fun!

At lasso-ing, oor lad's a hit—

In fact, he's got a " flair " for it!

Oor lad's in hiding up a tree—

But will Pa find him? Wait and see!

Four wee goalies—who's the best?—

Guess who comes top in the test!

Though Wull's in trouble as a rule—

Today he's teacher's pet at school!

Ten-feet tall sounds great, but see—

It's far, far safer being wee!

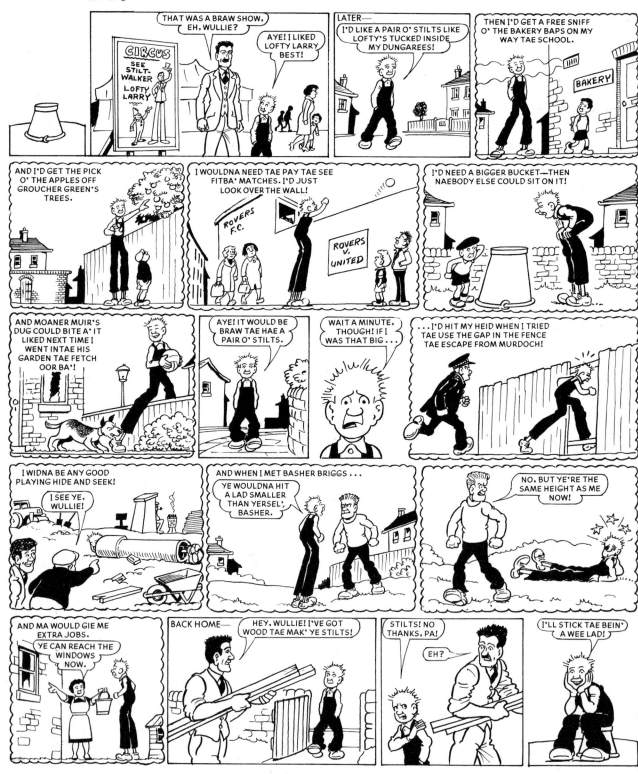

A fine safe seat? That's what he thinks—
But see that funny pail's high jinks!

WULLIE'S AT THE MATCH!

SMASHIN' GAME! BUT I'M TIRED WI' A' THAT STANDING.

THERE'S ONE OF THE ROVERS' DIRECTORS. I WISH I COULD TRAVEL HAME LIKE THAT INSTEAD O' WALKING.

IT WOULD BE BRAW TAE HAE A BIG CAR.

THERE'S A SNAG, THOUGH!

THE LASSIES MIGHT THINK I WAS A LAD LIKE JOHN TRAVOLTA, AND MOB ME!

A POSH CAR'S OOT, BUT ANE O' THOSE SEDAN CHAIRS WOULD DAE INSTEAD!

I COULD HAE A COMFY SEAT ON MY WAY HAME.

BUT KNOWING MY LUCK, IT WOULD HAE WOODWORM!

THERE'S ALWAYS A RICKSHAW.

I COULD BRIBE FAT BOAB WI' SWEETS TAE PULL IT FOR ME.

BUT BOAB'S HANDS WOULD PROBABLY BE A' GREASY WI' EATING CHIPS . . .

AND I'D END UP PULLING IT MASEL'!

HAME AT LAST. NOW FOR A SEAT!

ACH! MAYBE IT'S JUST AS WELL YOU CANNA MOVE, BUCKET!

BUT—

OUCH!

WULLIE! I DIDNA THINK YE'D BE BACK SO SOON!

I CAUGHT MRS BLACK'S KITTEN WI' YER BUCKET. I JUST WENT TAE FETCH HER.

YE CANNA RELY ON ANYTHING THESE DAYS!

He's no' just an angler—

He's a crafty wee wangler!

Here's a right—

" Hair-raising " sight!

A rabbit's foot brings luck, they say—

But this one fills Wull with dismay!

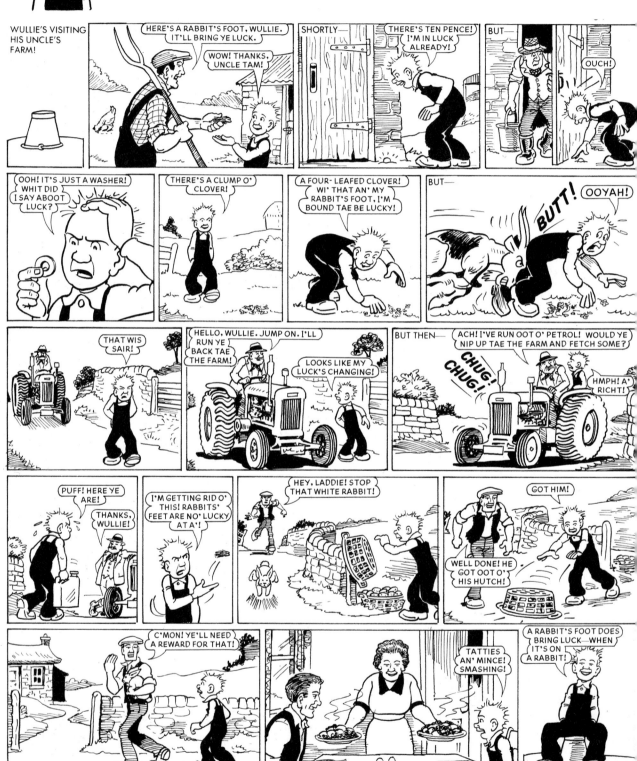

A two-wheeled hut—

Sounds smashing, but . . .

HI, ECK! COMIN' TAE THE GANG MEETING IN BOAB'S SHED?
NO, WULLIE! WE'RE AWA' FOR THE WEEKEND!

LUCKY THING!

ECK'S AWA' IN HIS DAD'S CARAVAN! IT WOULD BE BRAW IF WE HAD A MOVING GANG HUT!
BOAB'S SHED.

WE COULD GO TAE A' THE ROVERS' AWA' MATCHES IN A MOVING HUT!

WE'D NEVER MISS A GAME . . .

. . . AND WE'D SEE THE MATCH FOR NOTHING!

WHEN WE'RE AT WAR WI' THE GREEN GANG . . .

. . . AND THEY'RE PLOTTING . . .
LET'S GET WULLIE'S MOB!

. . . WE COULD TAK' THEM BY SURPRISE!

AYE! AN' WHEN IT'S APPLE PLUNDERING TIME . . .

WE COULD NIP INTAE THE HUT WI' OOR SPOILS . . .

AND MURDOCH WOULD NEVER BE ABLE TAE CATCH US!

WHEN IT'S TIME TAE CLEAN THE WINDOWS . . .

. . . AND PA PUTS HIS FOOT DOON . . .
THEY'RE A DISGRACE!

. . . WE COULD JIST TAK' THE HUT THROUGH THE CAR WASH.

YE'RE RIGHT, WULLIE! A MOVING HUT WOULD BE BRAW!

HELP! THE WALL'S COLLAPSIN'!

OOH! WE GOT A MOVING HUT— BUT NO' THE KIND WE WANTED!

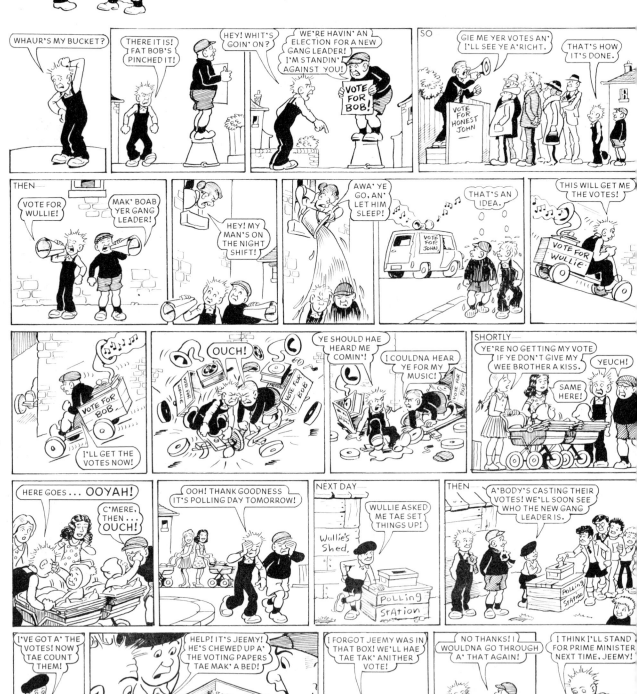

One sock for a foot, and one for a nose—

That's the way this swopping goes!

Wee Eck's ma fair lost her rag—

When she saw Wullie's racing flag!

At cutting grass Wull thinks he's fly—

But there's " mower " to this than meets the eye!

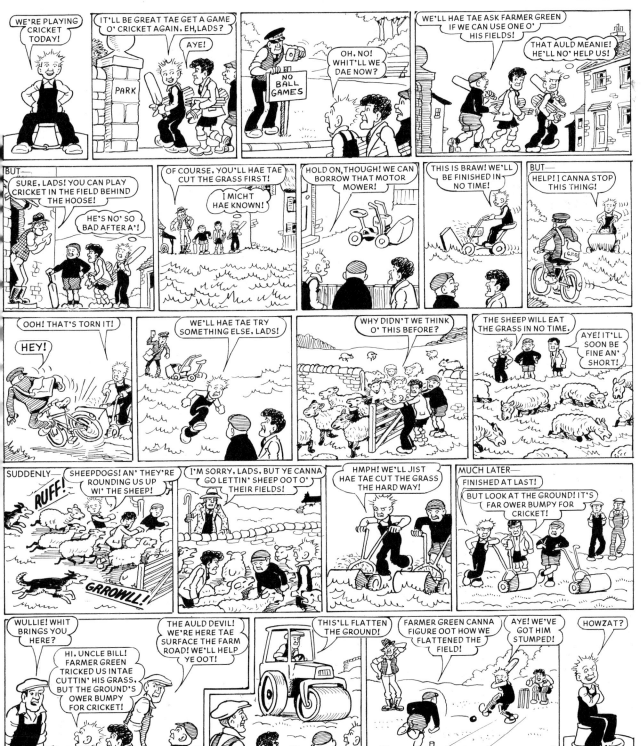

He seeks it here, he seeks it there—

He seeks that bucket everywhere!

Three lads go for a cartie run—

And they soon have TREEmendous fun!

Things go well for Wull until—

His sledge zooms BACKWARDS doon the hill!

When the snow lies deep and thick—

Oor lad gets up to every trick!

Fat Bob mumbles, Oor Wullie sneezes—

They're the victims o' each other's wheezes!

Here's some news that's really shocking—

Wull can't find a Christmas stocking!

Oor Wullie's got a grand solution—

He's found the perfect resolution!